This book belongs to:

....

....

Coloring fun!

call 9-1-1

Contact 9-1-1 in an emergency to:
- Save a life
- Stop a crime
- Report a fire

Word Search

E	O	H	E	L	P	N	P	H
S	M	G	E	T	O	U	T	F
F	D	E	C	A	L	L	S	R
T	I	M	R	H	I	A	A	P
H	E	R	O	G	C	I	F	H
Y	D	A	E	R	E	D	E	O
S	A	V	E	M	M	N	H	N
A	M	B	U	L	A	N	C	E
D	F	I	R	E	N	N	R	Y

AMBULANCE DIAL
EMERGENCY FIREMAN
GET OUT   POLICEMAN
READY   SAFE
SAVE   PHONE
CALL   FAST
FIRE   HERO
HELP

9-1-1 Safety Certificate

Help prepare children by making sure they can provide the information a 9-1-1- dispatcher will ask for details.

Name:- ....

Address:-

....

Phone number:-

....

Parents' names:-

....

....

Connect the dots and color.

Pattern fun!
Draw the next picture of pattern.

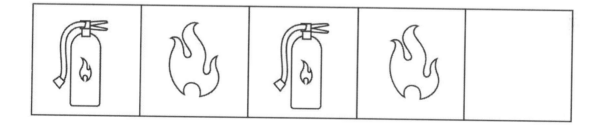
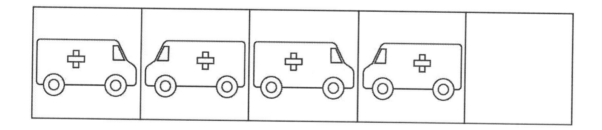

Help Nugget the skunk find the correct path.

Unscramble the words.

BUALANMCE ....

EYRGMENCE ....

TEG TOU ....

EYADR ....

VSEA ....

LALC ....

RFIE ....

HPLE ....

REMFINA ....

OLMICEAPN ....

SFEA ....

NPHEO ....

FSTA ....

HROE ....

Spot the 5 differences.

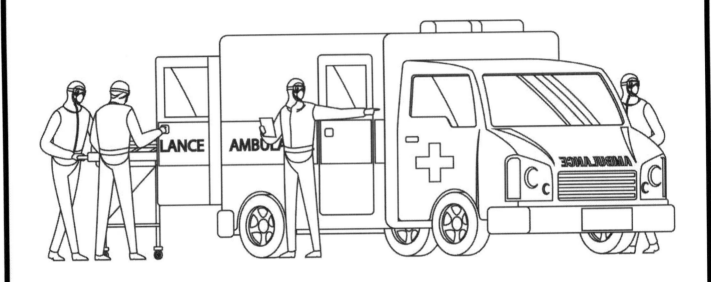

What is the emergency number?

Color the letter "A" in red color and write the number, what you find.

M	M	M	M	M	M	M	M	M	M	M	M	M
M	A	A	A	A	A	M	M	A	M	M	A	M
M	A	M	M	M	A	M	M	A	M	M	A	M
M	A	M	M	M	A	M	M	A	M	M	A	M
M	A	M	M	M	A	M	M	A	M	M	A	M
M	A	A	A	A	A	M	M	A	M	M	A	M
M	M	M	M	M	A	M	M	A	M	M	A	M
M	M	M	M	M	A	M	M	A	M	M	A	M
M	M	M	M	M	A	M	M	A	M	M	A	M
M	A	A	A	A	A	M	M	A	M	M	A	M
M	M	M	M	M	M	M	M	M	M	M	M	M

When we can call 9-1-1?

Put the right mark for the situations, we should ask help from 9-1-1.

| Your friend falls out of a tree and is hurt very badly. | ☐ |

| You see a stranger lurking around your house. | ☐ |

| You are home alone and you are bored and lonely. | ☐ |

| Your neighbor's house in on fire. | ☐ |

| You see a car accident where someone is hurt. | ☐ |

| When you have an argument with your best friend. | ☐ |

| Your dog is limping. | ☐ |

| You see someone breaking into a neighbor's house. | ☐ |

Match the shadows.

 Call 911

How to call 9-1-1?
Reda the sentences and put the numbers for correct order.

Know your address	◯
If reporting a fire or crime, call from a safe place	◯
Stay calm	1
Stay on the line until told to hang up	◯
Speak clearly & tell what help is needed	◯
Follow instructions	◯

Name these 3 people and color them.

Spot the 5 differences.

Word Search

L	I	N	P	R	O	T	E	C	T	P	W
H	E	R	O	J	E	U	C	S	E	R	F
D	V	T	L	W	T	R	B	L	R	V	I
C	M	D	I	S	P	A	T	C	H	E	R
S	X	Z	C	Q	R	M	W	D	J	M	E
T	A	C	E	F	R	I	E	N	D	E	F
H	N	F	S	D	H	P	T	E	R	R	H
N	I	N	E	O	N	E	O	N	E	G	P
R	C	A	D	T	F	N	T	A	G	E	I
U	H	U	R	R	Y	O	R	I	N	N	C
A	E	H	L	R	M	H	O	E	A	C	R
O	E	L	H	E	L	P	U	V	D	Y	I
L	A	R	F	N	R	L	B	M	C	I	M
C	G	P	A	M	B	U	L	A	N	C	E
L	E	W	R	E	P	N	E	T	U	C	K

CALL   HELP   POLICE
FIRE   PHONE   RESCUE
HURRY   PROTECT   CRIME
NINE ONE ONE   TROUBLE   AMBULANCE
SAFETY   EMERGENCY   DISPATCHER
DANGER   HERO   FRIEND

Help the policeman to catch the thief.

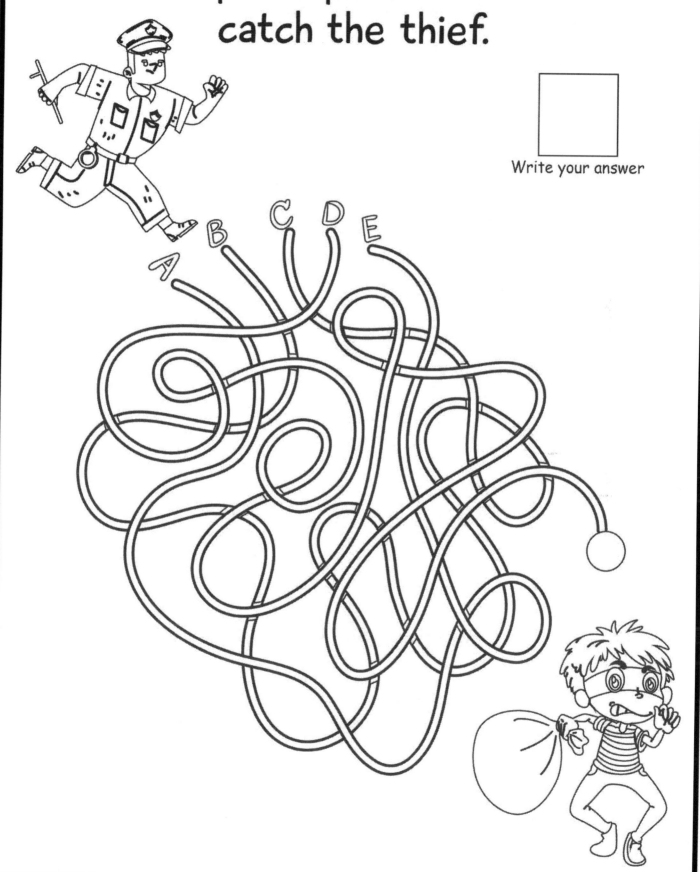

Help the ambulance to find the place where is an emergency.

Coloring fun!

Spot the 5 differences.

Pattern fun!
Draw the next picture of pattern.

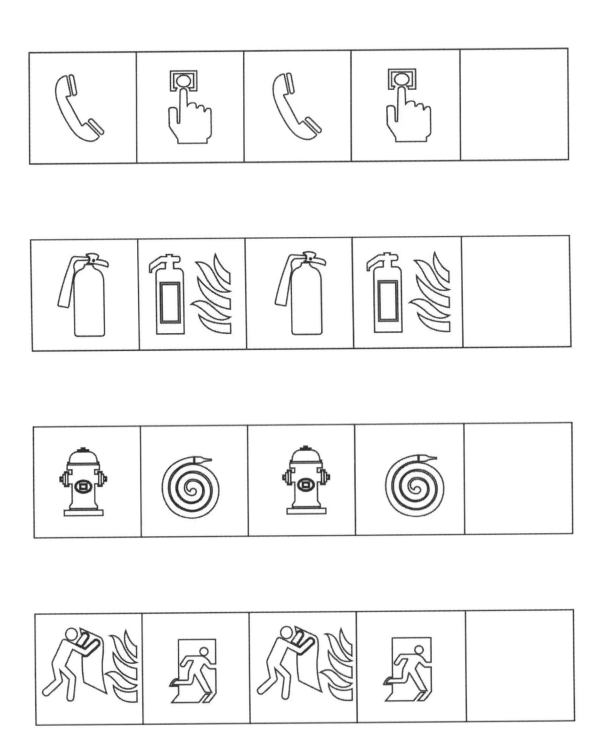

When do you call 9-1-1?

Color the pictures you think depicts when it's ok to call 9-1-1.

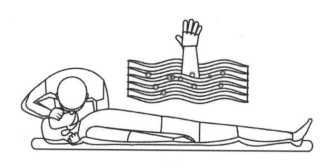

Help the fire fighters to find the place where is fire.

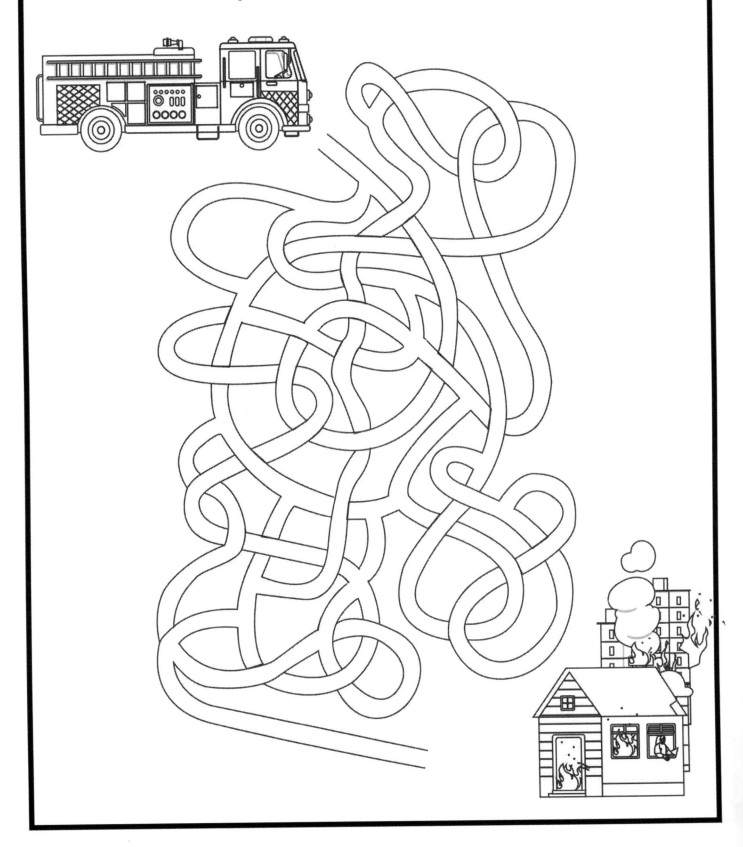

Emergency List

1). Your full name:

   ....

   ....

2). Your parents' full names:

   ....

   ....

3). Where do you live?:

   ....

   ....

4). Who do you call if you can not reach your parents? What is their phone numbers?

   ....

   ....

5). For a serious emergency always call:

9-1-1

6). If you get separated from your parents in an emergency, where is your meeting place?

   ....

   ....

Answers

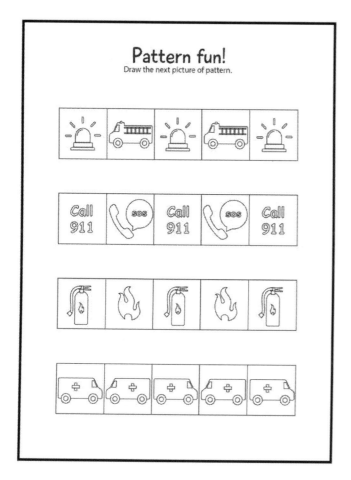
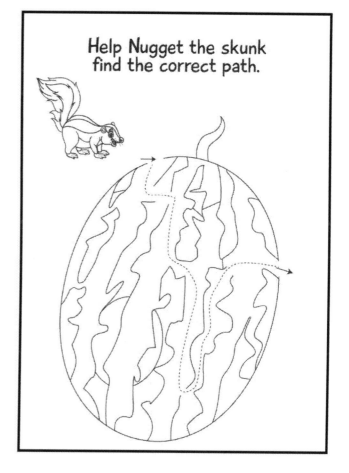

Unscramble the words.

BUALANMCE	AMBULANCE
EYRGMENCE	EMERGENCY
TEG TOU	GET OUT
EYADR	READY
VSEA	SAVE
LALC	CALL
RFIE	FIRE
HPLE	HELP
REMFINA	FIREMAN
OLMICEAPN	POLICEMAN
SFEA	SAFE
NPHEO	PHONE
FSTA	FAST
HROE	HERO

Spot the 5 differences.

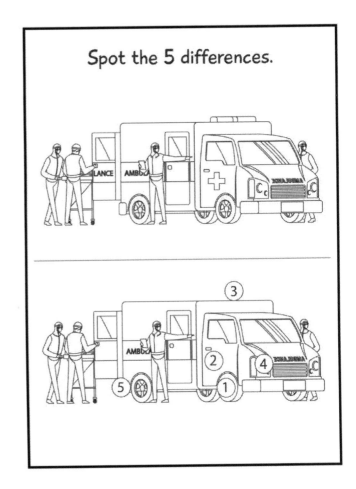

What is the emergency number?
Color the letter "A" in red color and write the number, what you find.

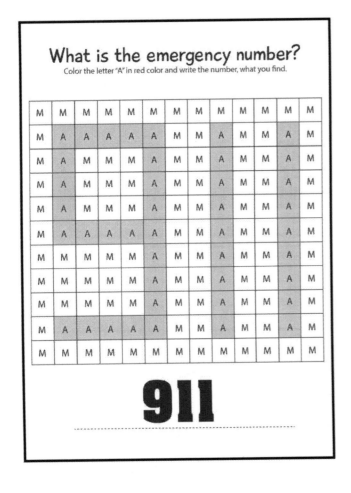

911

When we can call 9-1-1?
Put the right mark for the situations, we should ask help from 9-1-1.

Your friend falls out of a tree and is hurt very badly.	✓
You see a stranger lurking around your house.	✓
You are home alone and you are bored and lonely.	
Your neighbor's house in on fire.	✓
You see a car accident where someone is hurt.	✓
When you have an argument with your best friend.	
Your dog is limping.	
You see someone breaking into a neighbor's house.	✓

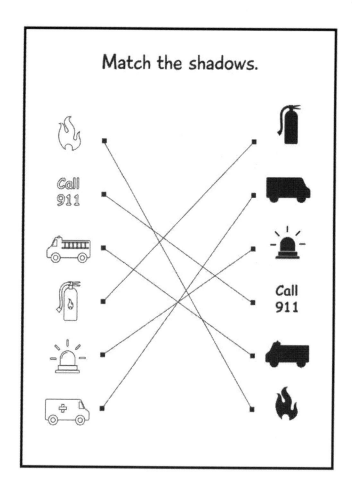

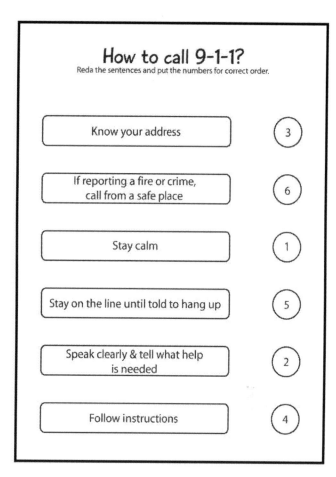

How to call 9-1-1?
Reda the sentences and put the numbers for correct order.

Know your address	3
If reporting a fire or crime, call from a safe place	6
Stay calm	1
Stay on the line until told to hang up	5
Speak clearly & tell what help is needed	2
Follow instructions	4

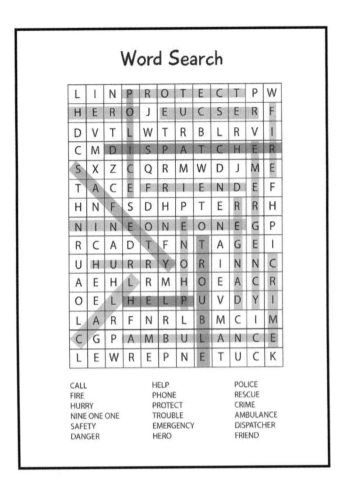

Spot the 5 differences.

Pattern fun!
Draw the next picture of pattern.

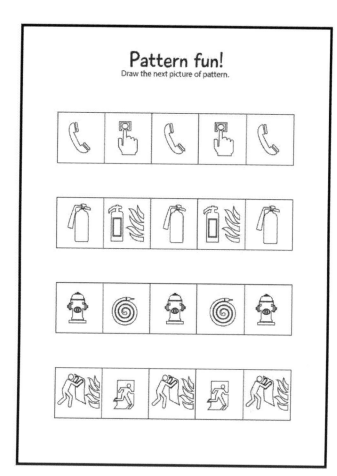

When do you call 9-1-1?
Color the pictures you think depicts when it's ok to call 9-1-1.

Help the fire fighters to find the place where is fire.

Made in the USA
Columbia, SC
18 February 2024